William J. DeRisi / George Butz

WRITING BEHAVIORAL CONTRACTS

A Case Simulation Practice Manual

Research Press
2612 North Mattis Avenue
Champaign, Illinois   61822
www.researchpress.com
800-519-2707

Contents

Acknowledgments

The authors wish to express their appreciation to Carl F. Jesness, Ph.D., research investigator for the California Youth Authority and Director of the Youth Center Research Project, and to our associates Paul McCormick, Rita Ramirey, and Tom Allison, Ph.D. We are especially grateful to the staff of the California Youth Authority's Karl Holton School, Richard C. Kolze (Superintendant), Cathy Filson Smith, Lloyd Bennett, Gordon Spencer, and especially to the youth counselors, social workers and teachers. We also express our sincere appreciation to Robert Paul Liberman, M.D., and to his excellent staff at Oxnard Center for Problems in Living, Ventura County, California; and to Larry W. King, Ph.D., Thad Eckman, Ph.D., Jan C. Levine, Nancy Austin and all of the people at Oxnard Center's Behavioral Analysis and Modification Project, UCLA Neuropsychiatric Institute.

Introduction

Terminology and Procedures

There is a continuing need for effective behavior change methods. Behavior technology, which includes contingency contracting, is one of the more recent and promising approaches to solving many human problems. It is also useful on an administrative level. Administrators are increasingly being required to justify their programs by demonstrating their effectiveness. Those who are responsible for supplying funds to human service organizations are requiring that services be conducted to allow for systematic monitoring. Contingency contracting is a counseling method that can meet many of these demands. It can, for example, be used to determine the need for additional staff training or increased case supervision of field staff.

Contracting is a technique used to structure behavioral counseling by making each of the necessary elements of the process so clear and explicit that they may be written into an agreement for behavior change that is understandable and acceptable to everyone involved. It is also a means of scheduling the exchange of positive reinforcements (rewards or desirable events) between two or more persons.† In short, contracting is a method for insuring that each party to the agreement—husband, wife, child, social worker, delinquent, teacher, probation officer—obtains an acceptable number of those rewards (including behavior change) that please him.

From the counselor's standpoint contracting is both a goal and a method. It is a goal because a new contract is the end result, the permanent product of each counseling session. It is also a method for reaching the other goals of counseling. The contract and its elements are the focus of sessions with clients; data collected in the contracting process are indications of the relative success of counseling efforts. And records of past contracts can tell the counselor when to abandon strategies that are unsuccessful before too much time and effort are wasted. Records of successful contracting strategies are also useful for planning other, similar cases.

In the crisis situation, when clients and their families are angry, the contracting process can shift the focus of attention from fault-finding and name-calling to problem solving. The counselor can direct attention away from each person's complaints about the other person toward positive changes in behavior that will be acceptable to everyone; he can thereby use contracting to defuse a potentially explosive situation.

Terms and Concepts*

Since contingency contracting is a behavioral technique, some behavioral terms and concepts are unavoidable. Those counselors who have had a liberal introduction to behavioral

† Richard B. Stuart. Behavior contracting with families of delinquents. *Journal of Behavior Therapy and Experimental Psychiatry.* 1971, *2*, 1-11.

* No detailed, theoretical introduction to behavior modification or learning theory is included in this book. Recently published books that cover these areas are listed on page 87.

methods will have no difficulty recognizing them. For anyone who needs a brief introduction or a refresher, here are the important terms and concepts:

Aversive

Unpleasant, painful, annoying, uncomfortable. Yelling and screaming are aversive to most people.

Behavior

An action a person performs that can be observed and measured. Walking, talking, running, reading, playing pool are behaviors.

Chain

A learned sequence of behaviors that are usually performed in the same order; all behaviors tend to be performed once the first behavior in the chain is completed. Getting dressed in the morning is a good example.

Consequence

An action or event that occurs after a behavior. It may affect how often that behavior will occur in the future. Getting fired is a consequence of being late too often. Getting a bonus can be a consequence of doing a good job.

Contingent

A statement of a dependent relationship between two events. It is probably less confusing to use depends on . . . instead of contingent. For a teenager, watching TV may depend on doing a certain amount of homework.

Generalization

Performing a behavior in a different place or under circumstances different from those when it was learned. The behavior of a youngster who swears accidentally at dinner, (e.g., "Pass the @!%$ salt") may be considered to have generalized from one setting (the street) to another (his home).

Mediator

A person in the natural environment of the client, one who can and will control rewards and keep a record of the client's behavior. The mediator actually carries out the program on a day-to-day basis.*

Punishment

Consequences of a behavior which decrease its future frequency. Punishment usually seems unpleasant, but not all unpleasant events are punishing to all people (e.g., yelling and screaming by mother *can* make the children behave badly more often). Punishment can be either giving something (a spanking) or taking something away (TV privileges).

---

* The concept "mediator" is found in the excellent book by Roland Tharp and Ralph Wetzel, *Behavior Modification in the Natural Environment* (New York: Academic Press, 1969).

Reinforce

To provide consequences for behavior in order to increase the likelihood that it will occur again or more frequently than in the past. This usually involves giving something, including attention, objects of special value, or privileges. It can also mean removing some condition that is aversive or unpleasant. A good example of this latter process—negative reinforcement—is the neighborhood bully who stops twisting your arm as soon as you say "Uncle."

Reinforcing Event

The opportunity to engage in some activity that is highly valued. Spending free time any way you want, such as hiking, biking or doing *your* own thing, whatever that might be.

Social Reinforcer

Usually approval or positive attention, but not infrequently other kinds of social behavior. Some people do bother you more often as a consequence of your attending to them by insulting them or getting angry at them. Insults and displays of negative emotion are social reinforcers for these people.

Tangible Reinforcer

Items that depend on some behavior; e.g., baby's bottle, food, candy, money, a new car.

Your Role

You should retain your present role, be it school counselor or police officer, while playing this game, and also suspend only a part of reality and behave as if you are supervising a limited number of cases. The book is structured to give you an opportunity to use contingency contracting in a situation that resembles the real world. You will be introduced to the basic principles of contracting and you will also be introduced to Roger, a young man who is made up of bits and pieces of real case reports. His story will probably not seem extreme to you; he would probably be called pre-delinquent in many programs. As you go through this exercise, you will find that certain elements are left to chance. Sometimes things will go well and at other times, even though you have done all that you can and the best that you can, chance will trip you up and you will have to change your tactics. After you have had a few weeks experience with Roger, you will find a section (Unit 7) detailing strategies collected from several programs that use contracting extensively.

Contracting Guide

When formulating a contract for behavioral counseling, it is *essential* to go through the following steps:

1. Select one or two behaviors that you want to work on first.

2. Describe those behaviors so that they may be observed and counted.

3. Identify rewards that will help provide motivation to do well.

4. Locate people who can help you keep track of the behaviors being performed and who can perhaps give out the rewards.

5. Write the contract so that everyone can understand it.

6. Collect data.

7. Troubleshoot the system if the data do not show improvement.

8. Rewrite the contract (whether or not the data show improvement).

9. Continue to monitor, troubleshoot, and rewrite until there is improvement in the behaviors that were troublesome.

10. Select another behavior to work on.

1. Where to Begin

You've Got to Start Somewhere

Behavior selection is the first skill to develop in contracting. When presented with a new case, you often have to select one behavior to work on first. This is not always easy since there are often many behaviors that need "fixing." Choosing the *first* behavior to work on does not necessarily mean it is the most *important* because the most important behavior may be very difficult to change by focusing on it directly. Running away from home is a good example. While this may be the behavior that upsets everyone, it is tough to remedy by singling it out. However, by finding out what behaviors have previously gone unrewarded or punished, and by seeking to alter those, the rate of running away may be reduced. The runaways may occur after a series of incidents at school or after family arguments. Dramatic changes in parents' behavior may occur following each runaway. Breaking down those events into their component parts will yield behaviors that should be given immediate attention. The first behavior selected may not be the one that seems most (1) _____ _____.

On the other side of the story, the youngster you are working with may be doing many things that are inappropriate, but which do not warrant attention just because they are annoying to some people. An example of this is parents who complain that household chores are being done too slowly by a youngster who is stealing cars regularly.

The first behavior chosen for the contracting process should be *functional,* and if performed more frequently will increase the youngster's chances of getting more of the natural kinds of rewards from those in his environment. If you can help him speak to teachers in a socially acceptable manner, for instance, then the teachers may be less likely to criticize him and more likely to reward appropriate school behaviors in the future. Behaviors that help a person earn more of life's rewards are (2) _____ .

In anyone's repertoire there are many behaviors that could be changed by a relatively simple rearrangement of the environment. However, not all behaviors are important. Selecting a behavior to change only because it seems easy to observe or to provide consequences for will more than likely prove a waste of time. The exception may be the case where you want to make doubly sure that success will meet your client's very first efforts, or when the client does very little he can be rewarded for; from there you will move on to other, more important behaviors. Keeping your shirt tucked in, sitting up straight while watching TV, and saying "man" three times in each sentence are behaviors that are easy to (3)_____ but for most youngsters they are just not very (4) _____ .

The report that follows will give you some of the information you need to know about Roger. More information about him will be included in other units.

1. important   2. functional   3. observe   4. important

Case Report: Roger

Roger is a 15-year-old whose late hours have increasingly worried his family. He has been picked up for curfew violations three times in the past six weeks. On the last of these occasions the police suspected that he was involved in a vandalism incident at a nearby shopping center (a description given by a witness fit him closely). When the incident took place, Roger was supposed to be at a friend's home, but both boys had left the house without telling the friend's mother that they were going. It is likely that Roger will be placed on informal probation after his court appearance.

Roger's school behavior has also been deteriorating. Never the ideal student, he has been called hyperactive or brain damaged. Medication prescribed in the past has not helped. He is currently in a class for the educationally handicapped because of his low achievement in reading, spelling and math. His scores place him two full years behind other students his age in these important subject areas.

In class he annoys others by moving around constantly. He does little actual work in school but somehow manages to get passing grades, although teachers report him absent from more and more class periods during the week. For this and other infractions of school rules Roger has been suspended, placed on a shortened day, or on a half-day schedule during different times of the school year.

At home Roger is less of a problem than he is at school. After much prompting he does his chores: picking up his room once or twice a week, taking out the trash daily, and helping his brother and sister with the supper dishes, although he still spends a lot of time away from home.

From your reading of Roger's case report, and before you meet him, *select* one of the behaviors below for your first contract.

1. Vandalism
   Turn to page 13.

2. Truancy and Cutting Classes
   Turn to page 13.

3. Management of Free Time
   Turn to page 14.

4. Quality of Schoolwork
   Turn to page 14.

5. Attitude toward Authority Figures
   Turn to page 15.

6. Delinquent Dress and Mannerisms
   Turn to page 15.

1. Vandalism

While vandalism is certainly an important behavior problem, it is probably not the behavior to pick now. First, it hasn't been established that Roger *is* a vandal and, second, remember the warning about giving in to the temptation to tackle the behavioral problem that has everyone upset at the moment. A third consideration is that vandalism, like other serious offenses, occurs so infrequently that there are very few opportunities for reinforcement and learning to take place. Try again. Return to page 12 and select another behavior.

2. Truancy and Cutting Classes

This is a behavior that often results in youngsters being put on probation or otherwise coming to the attention of authorities. The way many schools handle this problem is curious: they curtail the school day or expel the student. This action removes the youngster from the situation rather than teaching him and the school to deal with one another more constructively. Further, it also places the youngster in a position where he has many more chances to engage in troublesome behaviors. If you can assist the teacher and the family to motivate Roger to spend more time in school, real progress might be made. Good choice! Turn to page 17. If you think that you don't have enough time to meet with the teacher, then you should select another behavior. Return to page 12 and select one now.

3. Management of Free Time

Time to do the things we enjoy, either alone or with people we like, is a powerful attraction to most people. To young people it is especially important. Learning how to handle this time is one of the most critical skills a person can acquire. Roger has something to learn here, if our report of his behavior is accurate. You made a good choice in selecting this to work on. Turn to page 17.

4. Quality of Schoolwork

In our society we cling to the belief that good grades in school are indicative of good moral character. It may be true that the things most people must do in order to get good grades are incompatible with the behaviors that are called "delinquent." Studying to pass an examination can't be done if the person is out dragging the strip for action. But improving performance in school is the end result of a long chain of related behaviors, including consistent attendance at school, getting along with teachers and peers, picking out important information in class and written material, etc. But if the student isn't even present at school 80% of the time, the rest of this long and complex chain of behaviors is not likely to respond. It appears that Roger is doing very badly in his schoolwork. Only if you are certain that you can make progress by giving him some rapid success should you select this behavior. If you want to continue, however, turn to page 17. If not, select one of the other behaviors on page 12.

5. Attitude toward Authority Figures

Youngsters who are frequently in trouble usually have had bad punishing experiences with people in authority. Teaching them to respond positively toward these people—be it teacher, policeman, or parent—is a reasonable goal. It is also important if you are going to tackle Roger's truancy. If you can get him to relate more positively to some of his authority figures, then you may also be able to keep him in school. If you want to continue with this behavior, turn to page 17. If not, then select one of the other behaviors on page 12.

6. Delinquent Dress and Mannerisms

Wearing a watch cap pulled down tightly over his head, walking with a swagger, and growing a goatee may identify Roger as a "tough dude," but you shouldn't be too concerned with these behaviors. You could waste a lot of time trying to change them by attacking them directly. Go back to page 12 and make another selection.

2. Specifying Behaviors and Selecting People

It All Adds Up to Data

There are those who accuse behavioral counseling of lacking a soul, and like others before them the accusers have gone off to visit various wizards to find it. But the soul of behavioral counseling is data; and getting data is the most satisfying part of contingency contracting or of any behavioral counseling. Everyone involved in the counseling process gets frequent feedback. With a steady flow of good data success can be seen quickly, rewarding you and your client for your efforts. Lack of progress is also spotted quickly, allowing you to make changes in the system, and preventing you from spinning your wheels with an approach that's just not working.

The emphasis placed on the relationship between counselor and client in traditional counseling is well founded. Establishing a pleasant climate of understanding can only enhance your potential as an important source of social rewards. Data, collected systematically and accurately, help build an essential part of rapport—trust. Data also provide a focus for counseling. Reviewing the data on attendance at school, for instance, is an opportunity to apply praise and to demonstrate genuine appreciation for improvement.

But the question that often arises is, "I don't have time to collect data on more than one or two of my cases. How can I get good data and not get totally swamped with work?" The answer lies in the kind of data that are collected and in the people who can assist in collecting it.

What kind of data to collect? You have already *selected* a behavior on which to focus; now is the time to describe that behavior, to yourself and to Roger, in such a way that you both agree on exactly what it is. A precise description facilitates your collection of accurate, reliable data. This process is called *specification*.

The information you receive should be accurate; that is, the data should tell it like it's happening. One way of getting the real story is to set things up so that you also get *reliable* information. If two people can observe some behavior, quite independently of one another, and come up with the same numbers, then that one observation is said to be *reliable.* If these same two people make 50 observations, and if they agree on 45 out of the 50, then their data can be described as 90% reliable.

While reliability is not the same as accuracy, it is desirable to have reliable data for counseling with contingency contracts. But just to make the point about the difference between reliability and accuracy, suppose that we take our two observers who are now so skilled that they agree with each other 95% to 100% on their hundreds of independent observations. They see a performance by Mervyn, that master of illusion and practitioner of the dark art of magic. Sitting at opposite ends of a theater row, they make observations on Mervyn and his beautiful assistant. When the two sets of observations are compared, their agreement is still over 95% and their data can be said to be highly reliable. They agreed that the eggs, milk, oil, flour, and water *were* poured into the silk hat and that when the hat was turned over on the table, a fresh cake came out. Brightly colored scarves were drawn out of the assistant's ear, and when crumpled into ever-moving hands, they turned into doves and flew away. The data gathered under this set of circumstances can be described as reliable—95% agreement—but at least 50% of their observations are *inaccurate.* Special devices and slight of hand made illusion seem real. Fortunately for us most data collection situations aren't quite so difficult, and reliability will be one indication that the data we collect is believable.

"But where," you may still ask, "do I get 'observers,' and how, in heaven's name, do I set up these marvelous observation schemes? I don't think I have the time." Part of the answer lies in how you *specify* the behavior to be counted. If you describe *what* you want counted so clearly that a person completely unfamiliar with the case could read the description and go out and get the information, then it's likely that you can get the reliable and accurate data you need. Sound easy? Certainly. Now try it.

Here are some descriptions of teenagers' activities that are not well specified. Underneath each is a space for you to write another description that will be more specific.

Margaret should come in on time.

_____

_____

_____

_____

Elizabeth must improve her personal appearance.

_____

_____

_____

_____

Jeffrey's poor attitude toward his teachers has to change.

_____

_____

_____

_____

Donald's reactions to frustration get him into trouble at school.

_____

_____

_____

_____

Now compare your *specific* behavior descriptions with those you find below.

Margaret is to be in the house before 8:30 p.m. Sunday through Thursday; before 11:00 p.m. on Friday and Saturday nights unless she asks her parents' permission in advance to stay out later.

Elizabeth is to remove the curlers from her hair and comb it out before coming to the dinner table.

Jeffrey will answer one question each class period. An answer means a complete sentence or phrase of more than four words.

Donald, when having difficulty with arithmetic problems, will ask the teacher for assistance in a conversational tone.

Notice that these *specified* behaviors take into consideration many elements of the good news story: who, what, when, where (and how many). *Why* is deliberately left out: that question should have been answered, at least in part, by your *selection* of the first behavior to work with.

Specific Questions

1. Where does the behavior occur most often?

2. Where doesn't it occur at all?

3. When does it occur most frequently?

4. When doesn't it occur at all?

5. What do other people do just before it occurs?

6. What do people do just after it occurs?

7. Who is present most often when it occurs?

8. How often does it happen (per month, week, day, or hour)?

You will, of course, want to use your own words and perhaps some other questions. A detailed description of the behavior is the goal. By asking these kinds of questions, the client (in this case, Roger), and the people most important to that person (family, teachers, etc.), will have a better chance of getting the necessary specifics.

Now we want to get a detailed description of the behavior you have chosen to work on with Roger. Find the behavior below that you have chosen and read the results of the interview you just had with Roger. From the interview material write a detailed description of the behavior on page 24.

1. Truancy and Cutting Classes

"Oh, about five, six times a week I cut class whenever I can't take the hassle. I never do things good enough for them teachers anyway, so I split. Big Deal. Classes I like? No, unless you could call music a class. Mr. Duneen is the music teacher. He's okay, got a small rock group of his own. He lets me come to his room after school sometimes and he gives me a little extra help on guitar and drums. When do I split? Mostly third and fifth periods—reading and math. But sometimes I ditch the whole day. I get hassled about not doing homework or class assignments, and they make out like I'm dumb. So I make it on out of there. No, my folks don't find out for weeks. They put me on half days in school after I ditched so much. That's okay with me. I just hang around with some older guys, and we play tapes, play some guitar, lay down some sounds."

2. Management of Free Time

"My folks want me to hang around the house. If I do, they hassle me about homework and stuff. Besides, for every little thing I get put on restriction, two maybe three weeks. So I get out anyway. They really can't stop me. Ten ways I can get out! They don't want me to go out at all. Don't want me to be out after dark. I can take care of myself. They don't trust me. Treat me like a little kid. What's fair? Oh, nine o'clock on week nights, ten-eleven on weekends. But they won't go for it."

3. Quality of Schoolwork

"I don't know, the teachers bug me about it. Jump on me for every little thing. Other kids do worse things in school, but they pick on me. I can read okay. I can read the signs so I won't have any trouble getting a motorcycle license when I'm old enough. Mrs. Fan makes me read out loud, and she knows I don't do *that* too good, and the other kids laugh. I don't even bring books home. My dad works evenings and my mom blows up at me when she makes me do my homework and she tries to help me. Besides, it's always too much homework. Pages and pages—lots of math problems. My big sister Aileen might help out, but it takes too long. She's got her own stuff to do. I've had it with school anyway."

4. Attitude toward Authority Figures

"That SOB vice principal is out to get me. He told me he'd get rid of me. Well, not just like that, but I know what he means. He's out for me. Mrs. Farr has it in for me, too. She doesn't care. I just try to be funny when she calls on me and she really gets mad and yells and throws me out and the other guys really like to see her blow. And Miss Cannoli, she's not so bad, she gets bent when I don't talk nice to her. She bugs me five or six times a period. But I show her it doesn't get to me. I just won't answer her, you know, just clam up. She really gets mad then; but she's still okay."

Now write a description of the behavior you are going to put in the contract. Based on the information you've gained so far, make it as *specific* as possible. Write it out in the space provided below.

_____

_____

_____

_____

Mediator

There is one additional part of our system, one that is very important. You asked how you were going to get all of this done, how you could spend so much time getting data on just this one case. One answer to that very serious problem is to locate a mediator. A mediator is a person in Roger's environment (school, family or on the street) you can depend on to help you gather the kind of information needed. That person will also help with some other parts of your program. A mediator isn't absolutely necessary; you could handle the entire process, but there are several good reasons why you shouldn't try.

The first reason is that you will be doing too much work. The second, and more important reason for the ultimate success of the counseling process, is that by drawing other people who are in Roger's natural environment into the program, you are extending the range of the counseling system. Other people become counselors by getting involved and your power as an agent of positive change is multiplied.

But what makes a person a "good" mediator, someone who can be a real help to you and to Roger? First, the mediator should be a person who sees Roger frequently, someone in or near the place where the target behavior is to be performed. If we are interested in increasing cooperative activities with brothers and sisters, it would be necessary to enlist the aid of the parents, an uncle or an older brother or sister, or someone else who will be on the spot when the family is home and the kids are together. If it's a school behavior, a teacher, teacher's aide, a vice principal or someone else in the school's office or administration might help. It doesn't make sense to have a mediator who's never around to see the action.

A second quality of a good mediator is that the person be someone your client likes or looks up to; he should be respected. If the mediator has been associated with giving a lot of punishment in the past, then it's not likely that he will make a very good mediator now.

A third quality is consistency. The mediator will be reporting data and perhaps even delivering a reward to Roger. You are looking for someone who is dependable and who can follow instructions and understand the contracting process.

From the information you have about Roger, name the person you would select to be a mediator:

_____

Based on what you know about your mediator, judge his potential as a social reinforcer, how that person will act, and what effect he will have on Roger's behavior.

Strong — (1) Frequently in contact with Roger, (2) well liked by him, and (3) seems dependable.

Medium — Lacks one of these qualities.

Weak — Lacks two or more of these qualities.

3. Baseline Data

"What Do You Mean,'Just Count'?"

Since your target behavior is worded so that you (or someone else) can count it whenever it occurs, it is time to arrange things so that you can start getting the data you need. For a while we are going to be collecting data without a contract or any other intervention. This is called the *baseline period,* and it is useful for several reasons. Just how much of a problem *is* that behavior? Your records *tell* you it is and the people you've spoken to *seem* to agree, but—is the behavior *really* a problem? And if it is, how much of a problem is it? Is he really absent from all of his classes, or 60% of them? Does he always mouth off to his reading teacher? How often does he come in after curfew? How much later? Are the official reports on your desk accurate? The answers to these and other questions can all be answered by getting your baseline data.

The best way to get your baseline data is to start collecting it *without doing anything else.* No threats or preachments to Roger, no promises, just counting for a week or two and then, with the current data in hand, you can make some sound decisions based on objective information.

Data Collector

Now who will collect the data for you? Hopefully the mediator. If not, then who? You? A teacher? A friend of Roger's? Name the person here and give at least two reasons for your choice.

Person to help gather data: _____

Reasons for choosing this person: _____

_____

_____

_____

_____

Try to make things easier for everyone. The behavior probably doesn't have to be counted throughout the entire day. You can make a good start at helping Roger control his own behavior by focusing on one small part of the day. For instance, counting could be confined to one school period, during the evening after supper, during supper, or between the time school lets out and suppertime. Trying to count behaviors all day every day is only for the most dedicated behaviorists. It is not what we can expect from people who are just trying to be helpful. It is not what we can expect from most parents without a good deal of training, support and encouragement.

How will you obtain the data from the data collector? Check (√) one or two of the items below:

_____ Mail

Who supplies the stamps and envelopes? _____

_____ Telephone

If yes, when? _____

_____ Via a third person

If yes, who? _____

_____ Personal contact

If yes, when? _____

_____ Other _____

Details, details. But all very necessary to plan out ahead of time. And how frequently will you get the data to look at? At first, it is wise to check it frequently. Indicate below how often you will arrange to check with your data collector.

_____ Hourly

Nice work, if you can get it!

_____ Daily

Very good!

_____ 2-3 times each week

Fine.

_____ Once each week

Okay in many cases.

_____ Once every 2 weeks

A bare minimum. Chancy.

_____ Once a month

Watch out for trouble!

Let's review what you have done so far:

You have selected and specified a behavior that seems to need changing. Write it again, here:

_____

_____

_____

_____

You have enlisted the aid of a mediator who will assist you in the contracting process. Your mediator's name is:

_____

You have selected a person who will help gather data for you if the mediator can't get it. Your data-collector's name is:

_____

You have arranged how you will obtain the data. How?

_____

You have decided how often you will collect data. How often?

_____

It is time to look at some baseline data. Until now you haven't written a contract. The data you are about to collect will tell you if a contract really has to be written for the behavior you have selected. Wonder of wonders, we could all be wrong about some of Roger's behavior. Gathering baseline data will tell you the current status of the behavior you are interested in. If you selected:

1. Truancy and Cutting Classes
   Turn to page 32.

2. Management of Free Time
   Turn to page 33.

3. Quality of Schoolwork
   Turn to page 34.

4. Attitude toward Authority Figures
   Turn to page 35.

On each page listed above are two sets of data you could have received showing Roger's performance for one week. The data are graphed. Take a coin now and flip it. If the coin comes up "heads," look at the data marked A. If it comes up "tails," look at the data marked B. Read the explanation under each graph and follow the instructions.

1. Truancy and Cutting Classes

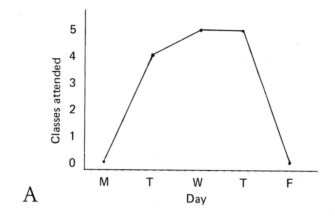

A

Roger didn't go to school at all on Monday and Friday. He attended a little over half of his classes this week, 56%.

Turn to page 37.

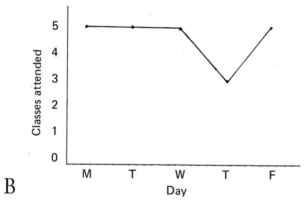

B

Roger attended all but 2 periods, for which he had an excused absence (dentist appointment). Last week his attendance was perfect, as it was for the last 3 weeks. Truancy is not a problem right now. Return to page 31, select and specify another behavior.

2. Management of Free Time

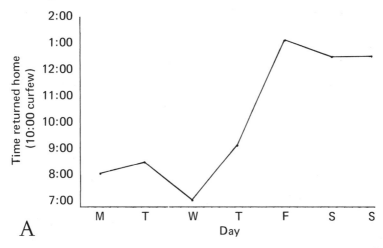

A

Roger was in before 9:00 p.m. on 4 out of 7 nights. On 3 nights he came home after midnight. Go on to page 37.

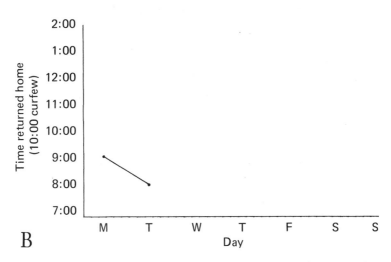

B

The person you had collecting data has turned out to be undependable. Return to page 28 and select a new data collector, then return to this page and read the instructions on the set of data marked A, above.

3. Quality of Schoolwork

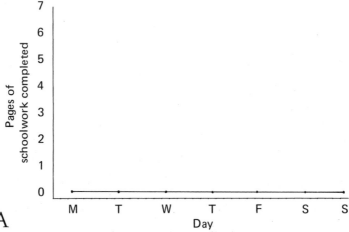

A

Roger has done no homework at all this week. Turn to page 37.

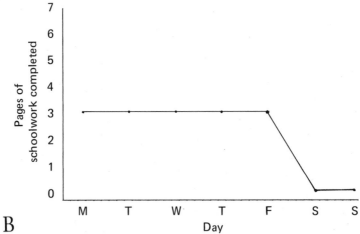

B

Roger has done 3 pages of homework every school night. Your mediator threatened Roger with calling you if Roger didn't do 3 pages of homework each night. Now they are both angry at you. Your mediator obviously didn't understand your instructions for taking baseline data. Go back to page 24, reread the section on mediators, and select a new mediator; then return to this page and read the instructions under A, above.

4. Attitude toward Authority Figures

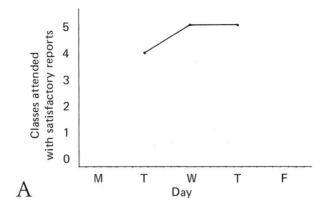

A

Since Roger attended school only 3 out of 5 days this week and on those 3 days he attended 4, 5 and 5 classes respectively, it is difficult to judge whether or not this behavior warrants contracting. From the 3 day's data it appears that his behavior was appropriate in 58% of the classes attended. Collect baseline data for another week. Read instructions in B, below.

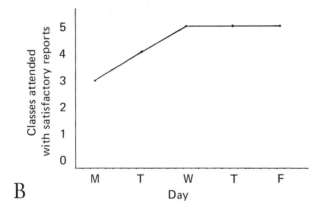

B

Roger was given a satisfactory report in most of his classes this week. He has resolved some problems he had been having with a few of his teachers, and for the present this area of behavior doesn't appear to be a problem. Turn to page 37.

4.

Negotiation
and Motivation

Getting It All Together

Negotiation

It's finally time to negotiate a contract with Roger. Note the word *negotiate*. Some people seem to feel that *imposing* a contract on a client will work. Such agreements are not contracts since one party hasn't had the freedom to determine the terms and conditions, and may even be forced to sign or accept it. One classic example is the school teacher who divided her arithmetic lesson plans into sheets of problems. She labeled these "contracts," numbered them 1 through 50, and handed them out to her students. Each sheet had 25 arithmetic problems on it. She gave them out at the beginning of the week, with instructions to finish the first "contract" as quickly as possible and then to turn it in. When a completed "contract" was handed in, a new one was given to the student. Each student was expected to complete at least one sheet each week. She couldn't understand why students were not turning in more "contracts."

Why do you think students didn't do more arithmetic problems? Give at least two reasons and check your answers with those given on page 42.

(1) _____

_____

(2) _____

_____

Motivation

Since counseling with contingency contracts is an incentive process, we must consider incentives for Roger. What is an incentive? Obviously it's something worth working for, something a person likes to do or to have or that he does frequently. Incentives, or reinforcers, are often obvious; money, clothes, good things to eat, etc., are incentives for performance.

However, there are some incentives that are not so obvious. Social rewards fall into this category. Approval from certain people can be a powerful incentive. Your time and attention, just shooting the breeze with your client for 20 minutes, may be a powerful reward. But for some clients a greater reward might be fewer and shorter meetings with you. If this were the case with Roger, you might propose to him that if he attends two more classes this week than he did last week, then he wouldn't have to come in to see you personally the following week; a phone call would do. Otherwise, he would be expected to come and see you as usual. For some of your clients your attention can be a reinforcer and you a source of approval. For others your absence can inspire positive change in behavior. This approach also creates a certain amount of humility in the counselor and it may serve as a source of solace when certain clients don't seem to warm up to you.

Describe two ways of using your attention as an incentive; then check your answers with those on page 42.

(1) _____

_____

(2) _____

_____

The strange and wonderful thing about reinforcers is their variety. While it is true that certain rewards will motivate many people, the human race is unparalleled in the different kinds of things that may be incentives. For most people money, free time, and transportation are very important. Approval and attention from others also motivate most people. But some people aren't into money and some people couldn't care less for the approval of others.

Name three of the most commonly used reinforcers, then see page 42 for the answers.

(1) _____

(2) _____

(3) _____

Sometimes the discovery of reinforcers is an accident. One 11-year-old boy was the terror of his neighborhood and school. The main complaint against him was hyperactivity: destructive, aggressive behavior toward teachers, parents, and peers. His behavior was rapidly getting beyond the control of his parents, who then had him hospitalized for observation. Extensive testing, both medical and psychological, showed no evidence of brain damage. But while at the hospital he became interested in tooling copper, an activity requiring some skill and long periods of sitting in one place. His contract, written when he returned home, had him earning copper-working tools and supplies. His behavior first became manageable, then exemplary. If anyone had suggested earlier that copper-working might be a good incentive for this boy, some counselors would have rejected it. But it worked. One of the worst mistakes you can make about reinforcers is to judge for another on the basis of what *your* reinforcers are. What's sauce for the goose may be poison to the gander.

It's also good to remember that the rewards you use have to be available when you need them. Trying to use reinforcers that you might not be able to deliver is worse than using no incentive system at all. Reinforcers should be readily available in the community and through legal channels.

Read the results of a further interview with Roger. During this meeting you tried to identify what kinds of incentives you could use to motivate him. You should have picked up on some hints in previous sessions. You might want to go back over some of that material after you read the selection below and before you write your first contract.

"Whaddaya mean, what do I like? Just hangin' around, I guess. No, the usual things, girls, yeah, I dig chicks. There's this foxy. . . . *Do* with girls? Hey, man, that's pretty personal, right? Oh, you mean, like goin' out and stuff. Yeah, we go to parties and just mess around. No, I don't take chicks to the show or to rock concerts much at all. Right. Low on bread and no wheels. Sure, I'd like to, but even if you go with somebody else, you gotta throw in some coins for gas. Gas is outa sight anymore. What else? Music—I'm gettin' pretty good. This teacher, Duneen, he's a good head. Really got it together. Sometimes he lets me practice in his music class, even when I'm not supposed to be there. I'd like to get my own guitar. I could use my buddy's amp. Might even pick up a used amp. Lots cheaper, too. Sure I'd like it if you could get my folks to go for some more allowance. Like to get a part-time job, too. You said once that you knew some people that might want somebody to do some things for money. . . .

"This is a neat office you got. You like the drags? I thought so, all them pictures on the wall. That's a kick, man, when those jobbies get off. Got down as close as I could once (we snuck in) and, man, that noise just about blew me away. And the smoke, man, this one dude had his engine come apart. Pieces all over the place.

"That your wife and kid? Nice picture. You take it? Real pretty shot. Fancy camera, I bet. I'd like to know how to take pictures like that. . . ."

How many reinforcers can you identify from your interview? List them here:

(1) _____

(2) _____

(3) _____

(4) _____

(5) _____

(6) _____

(7) _____

(8) _____

(9) _____

(10) _____

Now see if we agree on things that *might* be reinforcers for Roger. Turn to page 42.

Based on what you've read, select a reinforcer to use in your contract. Now you have all the elements necessary to write a contract that has some hope of succeeding.

Answers

Page 38:

Reasons why students didn't do more "contracts":
1. "Contracts" were really drill sheets.
2. There was no incentive for doing the sheets.
3. The student had no say about the terms of the contract.

Page 39:

Describe two ways of using your attention as an incentive:
1. Give 20 minutes of your undivided attention to your client after he completes a full day of school with no cuts.
2. Tell your client he doesn't have to come to see you personally if he attends 70% of assigned classes.

Page 39:

Name three of the most commonly used reinforcers:
1. Praise, attention, or affection.
2. Money or other valuable things.
3. Privileges, or the opportunity to engage in preferred activities.

Page 41:

Following is the list of reinforcers from your interview:
1. Money from family.
2. Opportunity to earn money at odd jobs.
3. Records, tapes.
4. Tickets to rock concerts.
5. Your attention.
6. Drag racing materials, tickets, being taken to the drags.
7. Attention and lessons from Mr. Duneen.
8. Transportation.
9. Electric guitar, amplifier and accessories.
10. Camera, photography lessons.

5. Putting the Contract on Paper

No Fine Print, Please!

The exact form of the contract when it is actually put on paper is almost unimportant if you include these items:

1. Date agreement begins, ends, or is renegotiated.

2. Behavior(s) targeted for change.

3. Amount and kind of reward or reinforcer to be used.

4. Schedule of reinforcer's delivery.

5. Signatures of all those involved: client, parents, mediator and your own.

6. Schedule for review of progress.

And, optionally (but strongly suggested):

7. Bonus clause for sustained or exceptional performance.

8. Statement of the penalties that will be imposed if the specified behavior is not performed.

When a contract is put on paper, it should not contain legal jargon that might be confusing. The contracts you write will seldom have any legal status; they are simply agreements between people and clear statements of how those people will behave toward one another. Even in those rare cases where a judge asks to be informed of the progress of counseling when a case is reviewed, the contracts have no legal status. Don't add "legalisms" to impress people with the importance of what you are doing. Make the wording clear, brief and simple. When was the last time *you* read a legal document that you really understood?

On the next two pages are some examples of clearly written contracts. You may want to design your own, but remember: the form is less important than the content.

Sample Contract

Effective Dates: From July 15 to July 22.

We, the undersigned parties, agree to perform the following behaviors:

If Roger will attend at least 3 of his assigned classes each day this week. Then Mr. Halpern will do the following for Roger: He will allow him to help in his store (3 hours per day @ $2/hour).

Bonus: For every 2 classes Roger attends over and above the 15 classes specified in the contract, Mr. Halpern will give him a pass good for one free hamburger and a soft drink.

Penalty: If Roger misses 2 or more days of school, he will lose his weekend late-night privileges for one week.

_____

(Roger)

_____

(Mr. Halpern)

_____

(Dr. Skeener, Counselor)

This contract will be reviewed one week from date of agreement.

Sample Contract 2

Effective Dates: From July 15 to July 22.

We, the undersigned parties, agree to perform the following behaviors:

If Roger will take part in two 30 minute role playing sessions this week (on Tuesday, 3:45 p.m. and Friday, 3:45 p.m.)

Then Dr. Skeener will discuss any subject of Roger's choice for 30 minutes following each session.

Bonus: If Roger has written down an example of a situation he wants to rehearse at each session, he can earn 10 minutes sailing on Dr. Skeener's catamaran. Each situation is worth 10 minutes (up to 6 per week).

Penalty: For each minute Roger is late, he loses 2 minutes of sailing time.

_____

(Roger)

_____

(Dr. Skeener, Counselor)

This contract will be reviewed one week from date of agreement.

Now write your own contract for Roger. If you put in a penalty clause, be sure you don't make the penalty so severe or long-lasting that it will interfere with future good performance or make the counseling process aversive for everyone.

46

Contract

Effective Dates: From _____ to _____ .

We, the undersigned parties, agree to perform the following behaviors:

If _____   then _____

_____   _____

_____   _____

If _____   then _____

_____   _____

_____   _____

If _____   then _____

_____   _____

_____   _____

Bonus: _____

_____

Penalty: _____

_____

Signed   _____

Signed   _____

Signed   _____

Signed   _____

This contract will be reviewed in 2 weeks from date of agreement.

Instructions

Good. Your contract is on paper, and hopefully everyone in your carefully constructed counseling system knows what is expected of him. Let us assume that your contract has been in effect for a week; it is time to check the results. Turn to the page indicated below for the behavior you are targeting and then follow the instructions for collecting your first set of outcome data. You will discover just how your well-laid plans turned out.

1. Truancy and Cutting Classes
   Turn to page 49.

2. Management of Free Time
   Turn to pages 50-51.

3. Quality of Schoolwork
   Turn to pages 52-53.

4. Attitude toward Authority Figures
   Turn to pages 54-55.

Some graphs will refer you to page 43 to refresh your memory; others will refer you to the blank contract on page 47. When you are finished writing your contracts, go on to Unit 6.

1. Truancy and Cutting Classes

Below are two sets of data you could have received, showing one week's performance by Roger. Take a coin and flip it. If it comes up "heads," graph A represents your data. If it comes up "tails," graph B is yours. Read the explanation under the graph and follow the instructions.

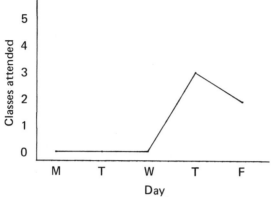

A

Roger made 5 out of a possible 25 classes this week. Somehow the contract doesn't seem to be controlling much behavior. Turn to page 57 and read the unit on trouble-shooting before writing your next contract.

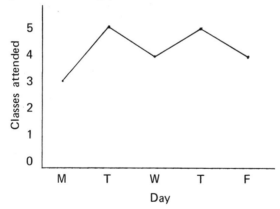

B

Roger attended 21 out of 25 classes this week. Good performance for a youngster who only attended 14 out of 25 last week. You've done a fine job. Turn to page 43 and write your next contract.

2. Management of Free Time

Below are two sets of data you could have received, showing one week's performance. Take a coin and flip it. If it comes up "heads," graph A represents your data. If it comes up "tails," graph B is yours. Read the explanation under the graph and follow the instructions.

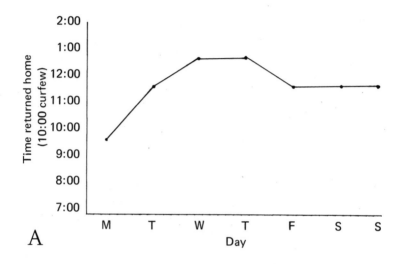

A

Roger didn't come home until after 11:00 p.m. on 4 out of 5 school nights. He didn't return home until after midnight on 2 occasions. Turn to page 57 and read the unit on trouble-shooting before writing your next contract.

Management of Free Time
continued

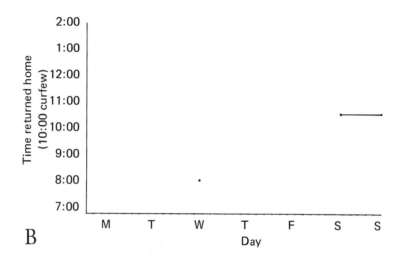

B

Data collection has been a real hassle here. There are only 3 nights for which we have good information. The person who is collecting your data has been undependable. Roger reports that he was in before 9:30 p.m. on each of the "missing" nights. Somehow, it is plausible that he is trying. Turn to page 43 and write your next contract. Also, contact the person who is collecting your data and give him a little encouragement.

3. Quality of Schoolwork

Below are two sets of data you could have received, showing one week's performance. Take a coin and flip it. If it comes up "heads," graph A represents your data. If it comes up "tails," graph B is yours. Read the explanation under the graph and follow the instructions.

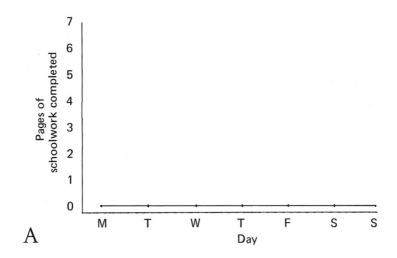

A

Roger hasn't done any schoolwork this week. One problem is that his attendance has been very poor. The vice principal says if his attendance doesn't improve next week, Roger will be suspended (peculiar logic, but that's life!). The vice principal grudgingly admits that he will hold off on the suspension if Roger attends 50% of his classes next week. Write a contract with Roger for attendance on page 47.

Quality of Schoolwork
continued

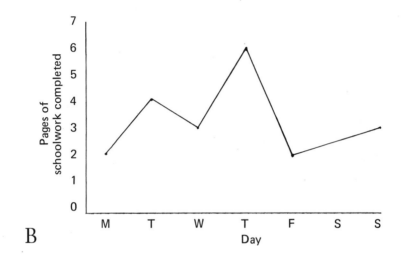

B

Roger has completed 20 pages of homework without threats. Your mediator has applied a new contingency. Roger may stay out 30 minutes (beginning 8:00 p.m.) for each full page of assignments completed that evening. Your mediator is a sharp cookie. Congratulate him and return to page 43 to write your next contract.

4. Attitude toward Authority Figures

Below are two sets of data you could have received, showing one week's performance. Take a coin and flip it. If it comes up "heads," graph A represents your data. If it comes up "tails," graph B is yours. Read the explanation under the graph and follow the instructions.

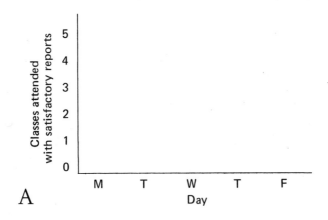

A

No data was collected this week. Roger's homeroom teacher was out sick; he was absent 2 out of the 5 days. The substitute teacher doesn't recall having any particular problem with Roger, but then she seemed to be suffering from an advanced case of battle fatigue, so it's hard to evaluate her report. Turn to page 47 and cautiously write another contract for next week.

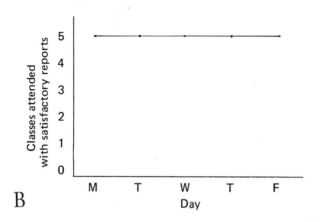

B

Roger's behavior in the classroom has been exemplary. Return to page 48 and select a new behavior to work on, then turn to page 47 and write your next contract. Be sure to include this area of behavior in the new contract also, just to be safe, and to give Roger additional chances for success.

6. Troubleshooting

Where Did I Go Wrong?

When things go wrong in contingency contracting, when progress is not being made or when the whole arrangement seems to have gone haywire, you need not consider pushing the self-destruct button. By some careful troubleshooting you can find out what went wrong and try again to get better results.*

Follow the instructions that you were given with the first set of outcome data. Find the heading that includes the area where difficulty occurred, and then make the changes that are necessary for improving your contract system.

* We wish to acknowledge Dr. Carl F. Jesness and Dr. Tom Allison and the staff of the Cooperative Behavior Demonstration Project, Northern California Demonstration Project (California Youth Authority) for their contributions to this section.

Troubleshooting Guide

The following questions may help you to spot the problems in your contracting system.

The Contract

1. Was the target behavior clearly specified?

2. Did the contract provide for immediate reinforcement?

3. Did it ask for small approximations to the desired behavior?

4. Was reinforcement frequent and in small amounts?

5. Did the contract call for and reward accomplishment rather than obedience?

6. Was the performance rewarded after its occurrence?

7. Was the contract fair?

8. Were the terms of the contract clear?

9. Was the contract honest?

10. Was the contract positive?

11. Was contracting as a method being used systematically?

12. Was the contract mutually negotiated?

13. Was the penalty clause too punitive?

The Client

1. Did he understand the contract?

2. Is he getting the reinforcer from some other source?

3. Do the reinforcers have to be reevaluated?

4. Has a new problem behavior developed that is drawing the mediator's attention away from the target behavior?

The Mediator

1. Did the mediator understand the contract?

2. Did he dispense the kind and amount of reinforcement specified in the contract?

3. Did he dispense it according to instructions, at the rate specified, and with consistency?

4. Did punishment accidentally accompany the performance being reinforced?

5. Did he stop mediating?

6. Do you need a new mediator?

Measurement

1. Have the data been verified as accurate?

2. Did your data collector understand what he was supposed to count?

3. Did you rehearse the counting task with him?

4. Did you reinforce him for *his* behavior?

5. Is the data collection task too complex or too difficult?

6. Should you try to get another data collector?

On the facing page you will find a blank contract. Write your second contract for Roger, then turn to page 62 for further instructions.

Contract 2

Effective Dates: From _____ to _____ .

We, the undersigned parties, agree to perform the following behaviors:

If _____   then _____

_____   _____

_____   _____

If _____   then _____

_____   _____

_____   _____

If _____   then _____

_____   _____

_____   _____

Bonus: _____

_____

Penalty: _____

_____

_____
(Client)

_____
(Mediator)

_____
(Counselor

This contract will be reviewed in 2 weeks from date of agreement.

Now that you've had another chance at this contracting business, try to collect some more data. Another week has gone by. It's time to see if all this hard work has been getting you anything but writer's cramp.

1. Truancy and Cutting Classes
   Turn to page 63.

2. Management of Free Time
   Turn to page 64.

3. Quality of Schoolwork
   Turn to page 65.

4. Attitude toward Authority Figures
   Turn to page 66.

Compare the data with that collected in the baseline and first outcome phases. Has there been any improvement? Are you satisfied? You should be thinking about the next contract you will negotiate with Roger. To repeat, one of the most important rules of contracting is that the process be used systematically, and not just when your client's behavior gets so intolerable that you just *have* to do something drastic. Doing nothing would be better in the long run, because if a crisis situation is the point at which you begin to give the attention needed for good contracting, then you may be rewarding very inappropriate behavior.

1. Truancy and Cutting Classes

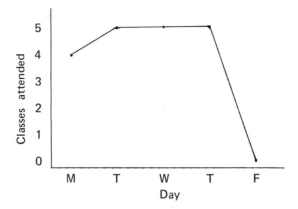

Roger attended 19 out of 25 classes this week, a bit over 75%. It would have been better but it seems as if he took Friday off. At least the attendance clerk doesn't seem to have any record of his being around on that day. It's good to remember to *praise* him first for the good work he's done, then bring up areas for possible improvement. One thing you might do for next week is to throw in a bonus for attending 5 days, at least 4 classes each day. Or, a penalty clause could be used to discourage days of non-attendance. In any event, you have done well. What other behavior of Roger's might be added to next week's contract? Return to page 62 and select another behavior. Well done!

2. Management of Free Time

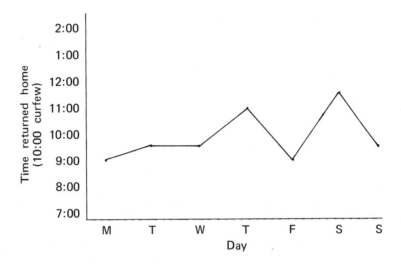

Roger returned home before 9:30 p.m. on 4 out of 5 school nights. On Thursday evening he said he was with Mike Monkston and Sid Bryan at Sid's house and he lost track of the time. Sid and Mike have been in various kinds of trouble before. You don't really approve of Roger's choice of friends, but you do appreciate his performance this week. For next week, you should talk to Roger and agree on a clause giving him a bonus for returning four nights consecutively on time. A new contract for continued good performance in this area should be written. Also, a new behavior could be added. Return to page 62, select a new behavior and collect base-line data.

3. Quality of Schoolwork

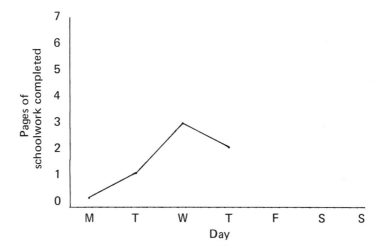

On Friday the vice principal had Roger suspended from school for poor attendance. You brought to his attention the fact that Roger has actually started to do some schoolwork, but to no avail. Return now to page 64 and select Management of Free Time to work on now that Roger will be out of school. Since he will only be suspended for two weeks, by the time you have a couple of week's data and some contracts written, Roger can go back to school and you can work on his attendance.

4. Attitude toward Authority Figures

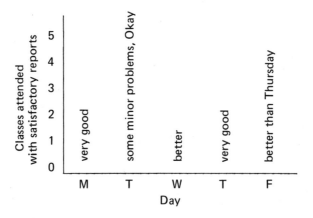

Instead of data, you have received general comments from Miss Cannoli who reports that Roger is much better behaved in school. He doesn't talk back in class nearly as often as he formerly did. Miss Cannoli is delighted to be part of the contracting process and wants to continue helping. In fact she has six other students in her classes who could benefit from your excellent work. Make a date to have lunch with Miss Cannoli. She's made you an offer you can't refuse.

Although the lack of concrete data bothers you, this area of behavior seems to be under control. Write another contract for this behavior, but return to page 62 and select another behavior on which to gather baseline data.

7. Sample Contracts

Strategies I Have Known

On the pages that follow there are contracts and contract strategies that are interesting either because of the ingenuity of the counselor, or because of the large number of cases where they have been found to be useful. While there are single contracts here, they are in the minority; contracting is, as Lloyd Homme has pointed out, most effective when used systematically.*

These contracts have been gathered from the wide variety of settings described in the introduction: a juvenile corrections institution, state mental hospital, probation office and community mental health center. They represent the efforts of some of the most skilled workers in the field. Most were not psychologists, psychiatrists, or social workers, but youth counselors, nurses, psychiatric technicians and probation officers, some of the lowest paid and hardest working people in the helping professions.

---

* Lloyd Homme. *How to Use Contingency Contracting in the Classroom* (Champaign, Illinois: Research Press, 1970), p. 21.

Each contract is accompanied by a brief description of the case for which it was designed. They are samples only; they should not be used verbatim without taking into consideration your client's individuality. As models to be imitated, such collections of contracts are useful. Specific treatment strategies are generally part of the oral tradition of a treatment setting. Therapists, counselors or social workers describe in broad terms how they handled this or that problem case. The specifics are seldom written down in a fashion that makes them useful; they are usually buried in narrative notes in file cabinets. The difficulty of retrieving written information that can be useful to others forces hard-working fieldworkers to rely on skimpy verbal descriptions and their own ingenuity. Treatment strategies, like the wheel, continue to be reinvented by succeeding generations of well-meaning people.

One solution to this problem has been the systematic review and collection of contracts for the purpose of constructing a data bank of useful contracting strategies to assist others who may be wrestling with similar problems. If such collections of good contracts are given to each worker and consistently updated, then the resulting store of information can save time and effort for both the trainee and the seasoned worker. The burden of originality in the helping professions is a heavy one, but one that can be lightened considerably.

Case Reports
Delinquents

Andy Harris

Setting: Community Mental Health Center

Client: 20-year-old male; chronic schizophrenic

Target Behaviors:

1. Take anti-psychotic medication as prescribed.

2. Attend and actively participate in day-treatment program.

3. Visit parents only on specified times and days.

4. Make restitution to owners of guest home for property destroyed.

5. Reduce rate of assaultive and destructive behavior.

This 20-year-old man tests the limits of community treatment. He is very active and resourceful. Attempts to work with him on an outpatient or day-treatment basis have been difficult at best. When he came to the community mental health center, his family, and the police of several towns, were about to give up on further attempts to keep him out of an institution. His behavior was unpredictable, partially because he took his prescribed medication sporadically, and partially because of the varied consequences provided by the people he came into contact with. Early in his treatment program he had assaulted a woman, striking her and knocking her down; he broke windows and other property in his residential facility, and ran down the median strip of a busy freeway, chased by a helicopter, when he became frightened at being stopped by the highway patrol.

After a year of intensive work, with contracting clear contingencies and consistent consequences as the main interventions, incidents of assault and incarceration dropped from almost once a week to one minor incident in three months. He no longer hounds his family with unreasonable demands and he takes his medication when prompted by his therapist or boardinghouse owner. He will require continuous supervision, but it has been demonstrated that systematic contracting that uses clear, fair, honest, and predominantly positive contingencies can sustain a young man with severe behavior problems.

Family Contract 1

Effective Dates: From June 5, 1973 to June 12, 1973.

Andy agrees to:

1. Take his medication as prescribed.

2. Attend the day treatment center program daily.

Ed, Ginny, and Mr. and Mrs. Harris agree to:

1. Provide board and room at Palm Haven rest home.

2. Meet daily with Andy to discuss his clinic program and problems in living.

Bonus: _____

_____

Penalty: _____

_____

_____
(Ed, Counselor)

_____
(Ginny)

_____
(Mr. & Mrs. Harris)

_____
(Andy)

This contract will be reviewed one week from date of agreement.

Family Contract 2

Effective Dates: From June 13, 1973 to June 26, 1973.

Family contract for Andy Harris; Mr. and Mrs. James Harris; Palm Haven owner, Ginny Ryan; therapists Ed Bryan and Gina Manchester.

Andy's Responsibilities

1. Attend clinic daily; arrive at 9:00 a.m. and leave at 3:00 p.m.

2. Turn in car keys to Ed or Gina each morning no later than 9:15 a.m.

Andy's Privileges

1. Andy will earn $4 per day, given at the clinic at 3:00 p.m.

2. Andy will earn 5 credits (tokens) in the clinic program.

Bonus: _____

_____

Penalty: _____

_____

_____
(Andy)

_____
(Mr. & Mrs. Harris)

_____
(Ginny Ryan)

_____
(Gina Manchester)

_____
(Ed Bryan)

This contract will be reviewed in 2 weeks from date of agreement.

Family Contract 3

Effective Dates: From June 27, 1973 to July 3, 1973.

Family contract for Andy Harris; Mr. and Mrs. James Harris; Palm Haven owner, Ginny Ryan; therapists Ed Bryan and Gina Manchester.

Andy's Responsibilities

1. Attend clinic daily; arrive at 9:00 a.m. and leave at 3:00 p.m.

2. Turn in car keys to Ed or Gina each morning by 9:15 a.m.

3. Attend meals at Palm Haven on time (8:30 a.m. and 6:00 p.m.) and abide by house rules.

4. Before visiting parents, call and ask permission.

Andy's Privileges

1. Andy will earn $4 per day, given at clinic at 3:00 p.m.

2. Andy will earn 5 credits in clinic program.

3. Andy may have a snack upon arrival from clinic, if he arrives before 5:30 p.m.

4. Andy may have phone conversations with parents.

Bonus: If Andy follows clause 4, above, for one week, he may spend Sunday of that week at his parents' home, from 2:00 p.m. until 8:30 p.m.

Penalty: If there are more than 10 infractions of house rules, Andy will not be allowed to live at Palm Haven.

_____
(Andy)

_____
(Mr. & Mrs. Harris)

_____
(Ginny Ryan)

_____
(Ed Bryan)

_____
(Gina Manchester)

This contract will be reviewed one week from date of agreement.

Family Contract 4

Effective Dates: From July 4, 1973 to July 18, 1973.

Family contract for Andy Harris; Mr. and Mrs. James Harris; Palm Haven owner, Ginny Ryan; therapists Ed Bryan and Gina Manchester.

Andy's Responsibilities

1. Attend clinic daily and participate in program.

2. Present credit system card (clinic token program) for review by Ed or Gina.

3. Before visiting parents, call and ask permission.

4. Save and deliver $20 to District Attorney's office before July 17, to pay overdue restitution.

5. Earn credits in clinic program at the rate of 5 per day.

Andy's Privileges

1. Andy will earn $5 each day.

2. Andy will earn $5 each day.

3. Andy may have phone conversation with parents.

4. Remain free (out of jail).

5. Andy may watch television each night after earning 50 credits.

Bonus: If Andy earns 450 credits in 10 successive days at the clinic, he may take his medication orally rather than by injection.

Penalty: If there are more than 10 infractions of the house rules, Andy will not be allowed to live at Palm Haven.

_____
(Andy)

_____
(Mr. & Mrs. Harris)

_____
(Ginny Ryan)

_____
(Ed Bryan)

_____
(Gina Manchester)

This contract will be reviewed in 2 weeks from date of agreement.

Brian

Setting: Correctional Institution for Delinquent Boys

Client: 13-year-old boy, committed as being "beyond the control of parents"

Target Behaviors:

1. Increase tolerance to taunting, teasing or other annoyances.

2. Decrease rate of assaultive, destructive, tantrum behavior.

This contract strategy was developed to assist in the counseling of those youths in a state juvenile corrections institution who find themselves at the low end of the pecking order. It was originally designed for Brian, a 13-year-old who was smaller than most of the boys in his living unit which housed 33 boys, ages 11-14.

Brian was not committed to the institution for criminal behavior, but rather for those behaviors that occur because parental supervision is lacking. To say that his home was chaotic would be a masterpiece of understatement.

One of his major problems in the institution was his inappropriate response to teasing by other boys who were amused at his spectacular loss of temper. They called him "Mouse" because of his high-pitched voice, and they sometimes aped his actions. He would respond usually by screaming and yelling, then by throwing shoes, rocks or any objects close at hand, and less frequently by attacking his tormentors.

In this institution points were given for appropriate behavior, and were redeemable for privileges and small items of value. The date of release was also contingent upon earning a certain number of points.* Since this was a closed setting, Brian's assigned youth counselor was both data collector and mediator. Only the behavioral requirements of this strategy are listed below. Each contract allowed a week's time for completion.

Contract 1

Effective Dates: From _____ to _____ .

Brian will meet with Mr. Scott (youth counselor) to discuss those things that lead him "to blow his cool." Brian will write these down and number them in order of annoyance value. He will be precise, describing times, places and people in detail.
      Reinforcer: 100 points

Contract 2

Effective Dates: From _____ to _____ .

    A. Brian will meet with Mr. Scott to add further details to the list of annoyances.
    B. Brian will discuss with Mr. Scott his present responses to these annoyances and write down as many alternate kinds of responses as possible.
      Reinforcer: A — 50 points
                         B — 50 points

* W. J. DeRisi. Performance contingent parole: A behavior modification system for juvenile offenders. In McKee, J. (Chmn) *Behavior modification in corrections.* Symposium presented at the Seventy-Ninth Annual Convention of the American Psychological Association. Washington, D. C., August 1971.

Contract 3

Effective Dates: From _____to _____.

Brian will rehearse the least annoying situation described in Contract 1, and he will receive coaching in the different ways he can handle these situations.
        Reinforcer: 100 points

Contracts 4-6

Effective Dates: From _____ to _____.

These contracts are similar in that they concentrate on practicing alternate styles of response to stimuli of increasing severity. The youth counselor exposes Brian repeatedly to the things that made him blow up before, and rewards him with praise and points for his participation. When all items on the list have been practiced in the sessions, the following bonus is added.

Bonus: Brian will receive 10 points for each day he keeps his temper and there are no incidents of throwing objects or hitting others with them.

Contract 7

Effective Dates: From _____ to _____.

Brian agrees to participate with a small group of other boys assigned to Mr. Scott. He further agrees to practice with other boys who will try to make him lose his temper. He will respond in the following ways:
        A. Ignoring the "agitation."
        B. Walking away.
        C. Using verbal rebuke as well as A or B above.
        Reinforcer: A — 10 points
                           B — 10 points
                           C — 20 points
Bonus: Same as in Contract 6, above.
Penalty: 50-point fine for each incident of physical assault or destruction of property.

Case Reports
Attempted Suicides

Setting: Experimental inpatient treatment program for patients who are serious suicide risks.

Clients: Adults of various ages who have volunteered for the suicide treatment program.

Target Behaviors:

Family-oriented behaviors such as chores, baby-sitting, telephone conversations, involvement in family conversations, paying bills, drinking, and leisure-time activities.

Contracts designed to remedy a particularly disturbing behavior very often do not even mention that behavior at all. In the section dealing with selecting behaviors for contracting, it was stated that the behavior that made counseling or therapy necessary very often is one that occurs infrequently, but is quite disturbing when it does occur, or it is one that occurs at a time or a place that makes it difficult to observe or to apply consequences. Running away, criminal activities, and severe outbursts of emotion are all in this category. The suicide gesture or attempt also fits into this pattern. While volumes have been written on the motivation, causes and effects of this singular class of behaviors, it is sufficient to consider suicidal behaviors as an example of that more general class of disturbing behaviors that require careful selection if contracting is to be an effective tool in the counseling process.

The contracts that follow are all from actual case files of a hospital treatment program that deals exclusively with suicidal clients. Contracting and group assertion training are the major treatment elements.

Marie

Marie is a 17-year-old girl who often behaves as if she were 13. For the past two years she has lived through a blizzard of troubles. A relative introduced her to drugs and sexual misconduct. She has been in and out of various treatment programs, including a drug treatment program in a state hospital, and a home for delinquent girls. She has run away from home and these various settings many times. Five months ago she attempted suicide by overdosing herself with sleeping pills and also by suffocation. A combination of contracting and group assertive training brought immediate behavior changes. She is now holding a job and dating boys who are non-delinquent. Here are the contracts worked out between Marie and her parents; they remained in force for approximately three months.

Contract 1

Effective Dates: From August 5 to August 26.

1. In exchange for the monthly privilege of receiving one decorative item for her room (paint, posters, rugs, curtains) from her parents (not to be purchased from allowance money)

1. Marie agrees to bring friends home and to get her parents' approval before dating.

2. In exchange for the privilege of receiving a stereo for her room after one and a half months of babysitting

2. Marie agrees that, without argument, she will babysit with younger brothers and sisters when parents go out (shopping, etc.) at least once weekly.

Contract 1
continued

3. In exchange for the privilege of having time alone with a boy or girl friend without parents or kids around (she must ask her parents for permission one day in advance)

3. Marie agrees to keep phone calls to no more than one-half hour; she agrees not to talk too loud and only occasionally to have private phone calls.

4. In exchange for the privilege of not having her type of music "put down" by her parents

4. Marie agrees to enter into family conversations when relatives come to visit.

5. In exchange for the privilege _____ _____

5. Marie agrees to _____ _____ .

Bonus: _____

_____

Penalty: _____

_____

Monitoring: Mr. and Mrs. Lewis agree to keep a written record of the fulfillment of Marie's privileges and responsibilities and to furnish the completed form to Dr. Thad Beckman on Monday of each week.

_____
(Marie)

_____
(Mr. & Mrs. Lewis)

_____
(Counselor)

This contract will be reviewed in 2 weeks from date of agreement.

Contract 2

Effective Dates: From _____ to _____ .

1. In exchange for the privilege of going out to dinner or just being alone without kids twice monthly (Marie must be consulted concerning babysitting)

2. In exchange for the privilege of a fishing trip once per month without the kids (Marie will not be asked to babysit)

3. In exchange for the privilege of having Marie keep the kids quiet on Sunday morning once per month

4. In exchange for the privilege of having Marie keep the stereo down to a reasonable level when the family is watching the news (6:00 to 7:00 p.m. daily) and during special TV programs

1. Mrs. Lewis agrees to stop nagging Marie about her past errors and Mr. Lewis agrees to take Marie shopping once weekly.

2. Mr. and Mrs. Lewis agree to allow Marie one hour of privacy per day when she will not be called or bothered.

3. Mrs. Lewis agrees to stop going through Marie's things (drawers, etc.) and to prevent the younger children from going through Marie's things.

4. Mr. and Mrs. Lewis agree to take Marie out with them for an evening without other children once every 2 weeks, or whenever possible.

Contract 2

continued

5. In exchange for the   privilege of _____ _____

5. _____ agrees to_____ _____ _____ .

Bonus: _____

_____

Penalty: _____

_____

Monitoring: Marie agrees to keep a written record of the fulfillment of Mr. and Mrs. Lewis' privileges and responsibilities and to furnish the completed record form to Dr. Thad Beckman on Monday of each week.

_____
(Marie)

_____
(Mr. & Mrs. Lewis)

_____
(Counselor

This contract will be reviewed in 2 weeks from date of agreement.

Harriet and Mel

Harriet, a 21-year-old mother of twins, fits the current description of the unhappy housewife. Her husband, Mel, expresses his feelings to her very infrequently and discourages her attempts to express herself on topics important to the family. He expects her to fill a very traditional housewife role: keep house, raise kids, pay bills, enjoy his hobbies and be gracious to his relatives. She had reached the point where she had almost entirely ceased caring for herself and the family; she also had spent a few days on a psychiatric ward.

Harriet became progressively more depressed and, after her second unsuccessful suicide attempt (by means of a midnight stroll on the fast lane of the freeway), she volunteered to join the suicide prevention program.

The staff of the program took her through an intensive course of assertion training that helped her to express her feelings and needs and also taught her some negotiation skills. Contracting between Harriet and Mel began with the detailed contract reproduced here. The contract remained in force for a month, with each of the clients living up to its provisions to the satisfaction of the other. After one month Mel has agreed to enter into marriage counseling, and Harriet has made arrangements to go back to school. She now expresses her needs and feelings directly to her husband. While this marriage may not survive, at this point it seems hopeful that Harriet will.

Because of the circumstances of the case this contract has many faults. There are too many important behaviors to work on simultaneously. The behaviors are also of different kinds: management of free time, communication, money management, child care, and recreation. To make important and lasting changes in each of these areas by means of a single contract would take superhuman effort. In fact, this contract may have helped only by the fact that this couple were able to define and to express their considerable problems as well as some possible solutions to them.

Contract 1

Effective Dates: From September 3 to September 17.

Harriet

1. In exchange for the privilege of going on a family overnight trip once each month, Harriet agrees to begin the school application process, including getting a list of courses, setting up an appointment with a counselor, arranging for a babysitter, etc. Harriet and Mel will discuss progress on Wednesday and Friday evenings.

2. In exchange for the privilege of spending one evening per week together, Harriet agrees to do 5 household tasks each day from the following list: make breakfast, do dishes at 6:30 p.m., prepare supper by 5:00 p.m., change beds (once each week), sweep, dust, mop, vacuum (twice each week), do laundry (once each week).

3. In exchange for the privilege of having 4 hours of "free time" to use as she chooses, during which time Mel will babysit, Harriet will refrain from smoking during mealtimes.

Mel

1. In exchange for the privilege of having 4 hours of "free time" to use as he chooses, during which time Harriet will babysit, Mel agrees to call a family financial planning meeting on every other Monday evening (between the hours of 7:00 and 9:00 p.m.) without prompting from Harriet.

2. In exchange for the privilege of playing golf for 2 half-days each month, Mel agrees to engage in a daily, 10-minute discussion session with Harriet during which one or more of the following topics will be covered: child care, personal habits, recreation, plans for school.

3. In exchange for the privilege of having Harriet assist him in the task of his choice once each week, Mel will express an emotion or feeling he has had during the day.

Monitoring: Mel and Harriet agree to keep daily records of each other's performance on the Monitoring Sheet and to mail the data to the project once each week.

This contract will be reviewed in 2 weeks from date of agreement.

Monitoring Sheet

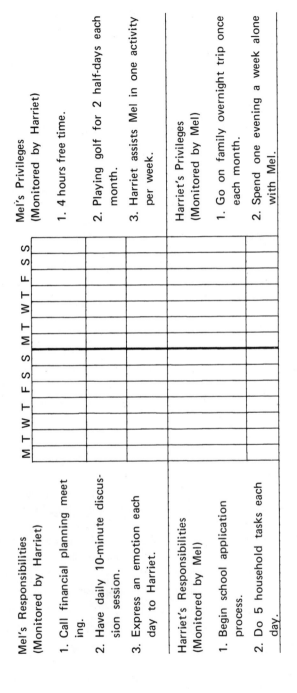

Mel's Responsibilities
(Monitored by Harriet)

1. Call financial planning meeting.
2. Have daily 10-minute discussion session.
3. Express an emotion each day to Harriet.

Harriet's Responsibilities
(Monitored by Mel)

1. Begin school application process.
2. Do 5 household tasks each day.

M T W T F S S M T W T F S S

Mel's Privileges
(Monitored by Harriet)

1. 4 hours free time.
2. Playing golf for 2 half-days each month.
3. Harriet assists Mel in one activity per week.

Harriet's Privileges
(Monitored by Mel)

1. Go on family overnight trip once each month.
2. Spend one evening a week alone with Mel.

Ted and Jan

Ted, on the verge of being divorced by his wife due to a multitude of marital problems, had decided on two separate occasions to end his life. By merest chance his last attempt failed. He volunteered for the suicide prevention program and entered into the intensive assertive training and contracting regime.

The amended contract (Contract 2) remains in effect. Both Ted and his wife, Jan, record data and report weekly to the project staff. The behaviors listed in the contracts amply describe the difficulties experienced by this couple. This contract also avoids some of the problems of Harriet's and Mel's contract. There are fewer behaviors to deal with, and the contract is thus shorter and easier to read and remember.

Contract 1

Effective Dates: From August 2, 1974 to August 19, 1974.

1. In exchange for the privilege of going out to dinner with Ted once each week (without children) and once a month (with the entire family), Jan agrees to hold a 5-minute conversation with Ted to review situations that occurred that day when he could or should have asserted himself.

2. In exchange for the privilege of being treated to a special social event (special restaurant, dancing, play, etc.), Jan agrees to go to bed nude one night each week.

3. In exchange for the privilege of 4 hours of "free time" each week without children, Ted agrees to engage in one 20-minute session each week during which he will exchange "I" messages concerning their relationship (e.g., "I liked it when . . .; I was very angry Tuesday because . . .; I really think we should . . . .").

Monitoring: Ted and Jan agree to keep daily records of each other's performance on the form provided, and to mail the data to the project once each week.

This contract will be reviewed in 2 weeks from date of agreement.

Contract 2

Effective Dates: From August 20, 1974 to September 3, 1974.

The provisions of the previous contract remain in effect. The following clauses are added, as agreed by Ted and Jan. This contract can be renegotiated at the request of either Ted or Jan, and at any time.

1. In exchange for the privilege of watching TV during supper no more than 3 of 7 nights each week, Ted agrees to inform Jan at least one hour before supper (usually 7:00 p.m.), and to discuss the day's events with Jan after the news is over.

2. In exchange for the privilege of having at least 2 parties at home during the next 4 months, with Jan's friends, Jan agrees to spend more time in sexual activity with Ted, having intercourse at least once each week.

Monitoring: Ted and Jan agree to keep daily records of each other's performance on the Monitoring Sheet provided, and to mail the data to the project once each week.

References

Becker, W. *Parents are teachers.* Champaign, IL: Research Press, 1971.

Hall, R. *Managing behavior, behavior modification: The measurement of behavior. I.* Kansas City, KS: H & H Publications, 1971.

Hall, R. *Managing behavior, behavior modification: Basic principles. II.* Kansas City, KS: H & H Publications, 1971.

Homme, L. and Tosti, D. *Behavior technology: Motivation and contingency management.* Palo Alto, CA: ILS Publications, 1971.

Homme, L. et al. *How to use contingency contracting in the classroom.* Champaign, IL: Research Press, 1969.

Knox, D. *Marriage happiness.* Champaign, IL: Research Press, 1971.

Lazarus, A. A. *Behavior therapy and beyond.* New York, NY: McGraw-Hill, 1971.

Liberman, R. *A guide to behavioral analysis and therapy.* New York, NY: Pergamon Press, 1972.

Malott, R. *Contingency management.* Kalamazoo, MI: Behaviordelia Press, 1971.

Martin, R. and Lauridsen, D. *Developing student discipline and motivation.* Champaign, IL: Research Press, 1974.

Patterson, G. R. and Gullion, M. E. *Living with children.* Champaign, IL: Research Press, 1971.

Patterson, G. R. *Families.* Champaign, IL: Research Press, 1971.

Schaeffer, H. and Martin, P. *Behavioral therapy.* New York, NY: McGraw-Hill, 1969.

Ullmann, L. and Krasner, L. *Case studies in behavior modification.* New York, NY: Holt, Rinehart & Winston, 1965.

Ulrich, R. et al. *Control of human behavior. I* and *II.* New York, NY: Scott, Foresman, 1966, 1971.

Wolpe, J. *The practice of behavior therapy.* New York, NY: Pergamon Press, 1969.